THERE'S A STEGOSAURUS ON THE STAIRS

Aleksei Bitskoff & Ruth Symons

QEB Publishing

Stegosaurus was a large, plant-eating dinosaur with a row of bony

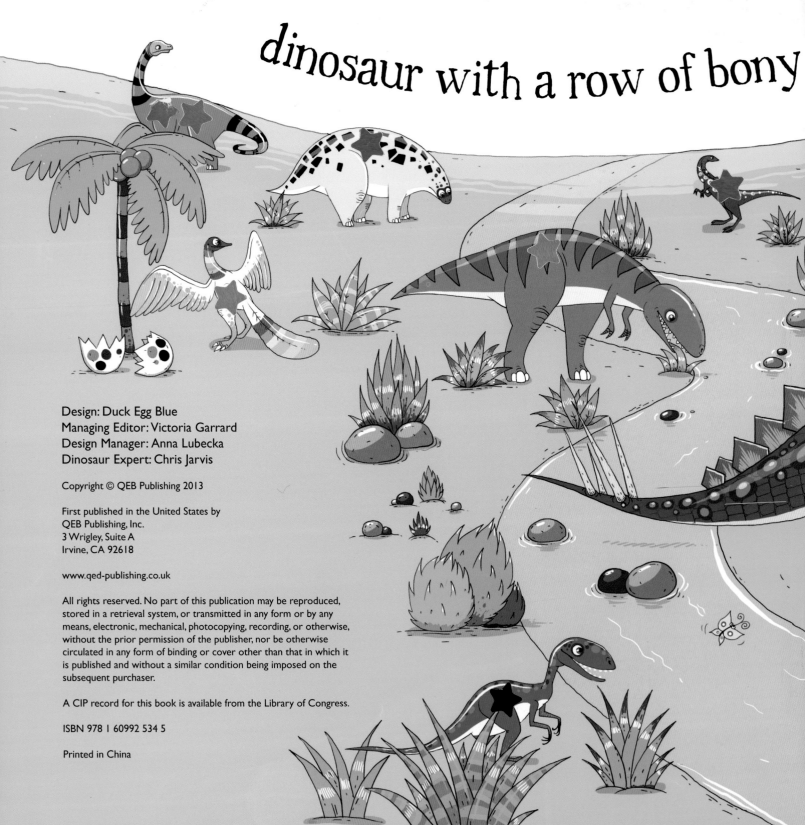

Design: Duck Egg Blue
Managing Editor: Victoria Garrard
Design Manager: Anna Lubecka
Dinosaur Expert: Chris Jarvis

Copyright © QEB Publishing 2013

First published in the United States by
QEB Publishing, Inc.
3 Wrigley, Suite A
Irvine, CA 92618

www.qed-publishing.co.uk

A CIP record for this book is available from the Library of Congress.

ISBN 978 1 60992 534 5

Printed in China

plates running along his back.

He lived around **150 million** years ago—several millions of years before the first humans appeared.

But just imagine if Stegosaurus was alive today! How would he cope with modern life?

What if Stegosaurus went to the playground?

Stegosaurus would need a big friend to balance him on the seesaw. He weighed almost 5.5 tons (5 tonnes)—that's as much as an elephant!

What if Stegosaurus went to school?

He might not be able to keep up with the other students. His brain was only the size of a tangerine!

What if Stegosaurus went on a school trip?

Stegosaurus would **always** stay with the group. Stegosaurus families lived in big herds, which kept them safe from predators.

What if Stegosaurus went for a walk?

He wouldn't fit on the sidewalk. At 30 feet (9 meters) long and 7 feet (2 meters) wide, he's as ...

BIG as a bus!

If he walked in the road, he'd cause a traffic jam. He could only walk at 5 or 6 miles per hour (8 or 9 kilometers per hour)—that's not much faster than you can walk.

What if Stegosaurus went to a party?

He could use his big, spiky tail to burst the piñata and get all the candy!

Stegosaurus had four big

spikes

on his tail. Each spike was as long as your arm.

And the Jell-O would really **wobble** when he started dancing.

Stegosaurus would weigh more than the rest of the party put together!

What would Stegosaurus give his mom on mother's day?

Stegosaurus could use his **sharp beak** to cut her a bunch of flowers.

His beak was

perfect

for snipping
plant stems to ...

munch on!

What if Stegosaurus sat on
a whoopee cushion?

Pffffffffffffffffffffffffffffft!

He'd be so
embarrassed, he
would blush—but
not in his cheeks!

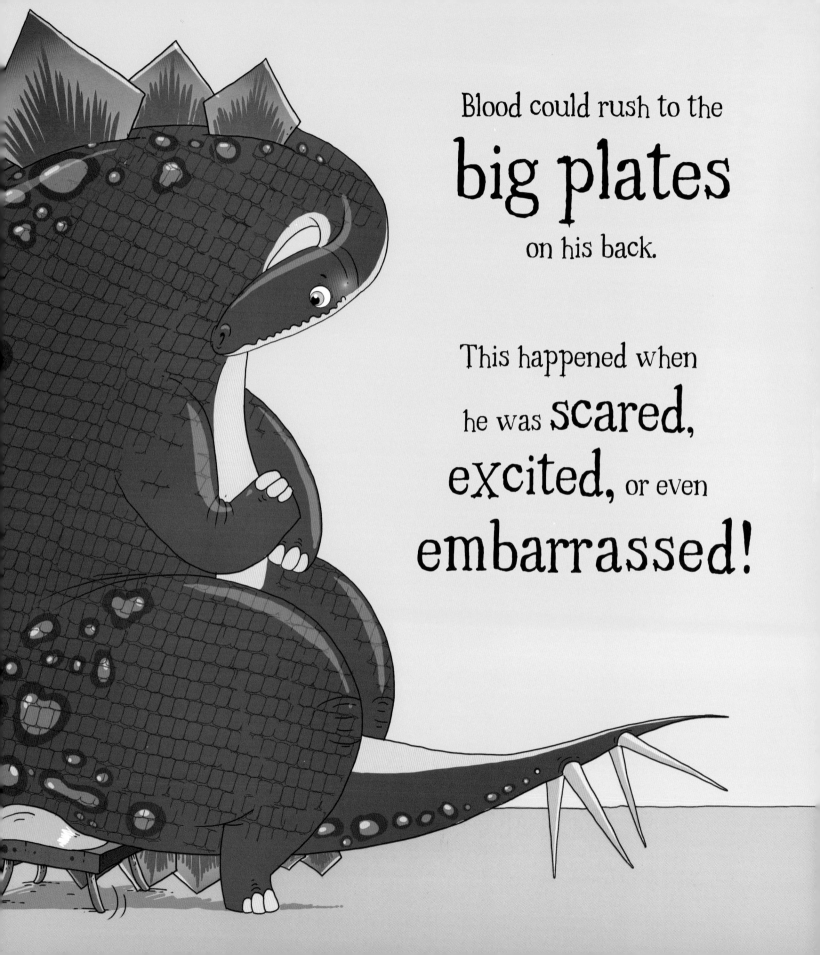

Blood could rush to the **big plates** on his back.

This happened when he was **scared, excited,** or even **embarrassed!**

What if Stegosaurus went to the grocery store?

He could sniff out the ripest, yummiest fruit.

Stegosaurus had an **amazing** sense of smell ...

much better than his eyesight!

What if Stegosaurus was sleepy?

Stegosaurus would probably sleep curled up on his side, like elephants and other large animals do today.

He might also be able to doze
while standing on all fours,
like rhinos, horses, and
other animals still do.

Stegosaurus's skeleton

Everything we know about Stegosaurus comes from fossils—skeletons that have been in the ground for thousands and thousands of years.

Scientists can look at fossils to figure out how dinosaurs lived in the past.

This means that we know a lot about dinosaurs, even though no one has ever seen one!

X-RAY 11932897378943-268

MODEL No.: nx110005468   19531876431

tail spikes

long tail

long hind legs

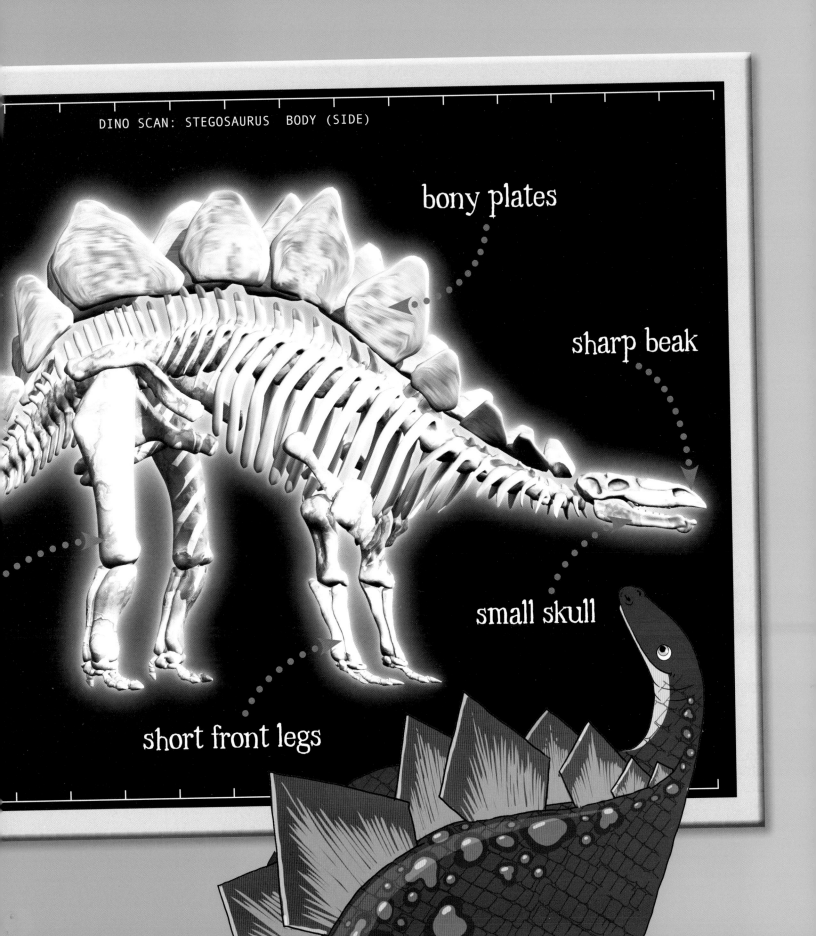

DINO SCAN: STEGOSAURUS BODY (SIDE)

bony plates

sharp beak

small skull

short front legs

COLORADO, U.S.A.
Most complete skeleton discovered, nicknamed "Spike"—1992

AUSTRALIA
Fossil footprints discovered—1995

WYOMING, U.S.A.
Back plates discovered—1879

PORTUGAL
Partial skeleton discovered—2006

UTAH, U.S.A.
Fossil remains found—2010

COLORADO, U.S.A.
First skeleton found—1876

PASSPORT

Stegosaurus

(STEG-UH-SAW-RUS)

NAME MEANS "ROOF LIZARD"
SCIENTISTS THOUGHT THAT HIS BACK PLATES LAY FLAT, LIKE ROOF TILES.

WEIGHT 5.5 TONS (5 TONNES)

LENGTH 30 FEET (9 METERS)

HEIGHT 10 FEET (3 METERS)

HABITAT WOODS, FOREST

DIET FERNS, LEAVES, PINE NEEDLES

234071209899872465435

S<STEG<<STEGOSAURUS<<<<<<<<<<<<<34263954302375<<<<<<<<<48273526291083546>>>>>>>>